50 Pancake, Breakfast and Syrup Dishes

By: Kelly Johnson

Table of Contents

- Classic Buttermilk Pancakes
- Blueberry Pancakes
- Banana Walnut Pancakes
- Chocolate Chip Pancakes
- Lemon Ricotta Pancakes
- Pumpkin Spice Pancakes
- Apple Cinnamon Pancakes
- Oatmeal Pancakes
- Whole Wheat Pancakes
- Strawberry Pancakes
- Sweet Potato Pancakes
- Gluten-Free Pancakes
- Vegan Pancakes
- Crepes with Nutella
- Buckwheat Pancakes
- Cornmeal Pancakes
- Ricotta and Honey Pancakes

- Peanut Butter Pancakes
- Cinnamon Roll Pancakes
- Sourdough Pancakes
- Carrot Cake Pancakes
- Lemon Poppy Seed Pancakes
- Bacon Pancakes
- Savory Herb Pancakes
- Chive and Cheese Pancakes
- Maple Syrup Glazed Bacon
- Honey Butter Syrup
- Blueberry Maple Syrup
- Cinnamon Maple Syrup
- Bourbon Maple Syrup
- Pumpkin Spice Syrup
- Strawberry Compote
- Mixed Berry Syrup
- Apple Cider Syrup
- Ginger Syrup
- Vanilla Bean Syrup

- Pecan Maple Syrup
- Orange Blossom Syrup
- Blackberry Syrup
- Lemon Syrup
- Chocolate Syrup
- Caramel Syrup
- Bacon and Maple Syrup Pancakes
- Pancakes with Whipped Cream and Berries
- Pancake Stack with Nut Butter
- Sweet Potato Hash
- Breakfast Burrito with Pancakes
- Pancakes with Fried Eggs and Sausage
- Pancakes with Greek Yogurt and Honey
- Pancakes with Fresh Fruit Salad

Classic Buttermilk Pancakes

Ingredients:

- 1 ½ cups all-purpose flour
- 3 ½ tsp baking powder
- 1 tsp baking soda
- ½ tsp salt
- 1 ¼ cups buttermilk
- 1 large egg
- 3 tbsp melted butter
- 1 tbsp sugar (optional)

Instructions:

1. In a bowl, whisk flour, baking powder, baking soda, salt, and sugar.
2. In another bowl, whisk buttermilk, egg, and melted butter.
3. Combine wet and dry ingredients until just mixed (some lumps okay).
4. Heat a griddle over medium heat, grease lightly.
5. Pour ¼ cup batter per pancake, cook until bubbles form on top, flip and cook until golden.

Blueberry Pancakes

Ingredients:

- Use Classic Buttermilk Pancake batter
- 1 cup fresh or frozen blueberries

Instructions:

1. Fold blueberries gently into batter just before cooking.
2. Cook pancakes as usual.

Banana Walnut Pancakes

Ingredients:

- Use Classic Buttermilk Pancake batter
- 1 ripe banana, mashed
- ½ cup chopped walnuts

Instructions:

1. Mix mashed banana into batter.
2. Fold in walnuts gently.
3. Cook pancakes on griddle as usual.

Chocolate Chip Pancakes

Ingredients:

- Use Classic Buttermilk Pancake batter
- ½ cup chocolate chips

Instructions:

1. Fold chocolate chips into batter just before cooking.
2. Cook pancakes as usual.

Lemon Ricotta Pancakes

Ingredients:

- 1 cup all-purpose flour
- 1 tbsp sugar
- 1 tsp baking powder
- ½ tsp baking soda
- ¼ tsp salt
- 1 cup ricotta cheese
- 1 cup buttermilk
- 2 large eggs
- Zest of 1 lemon
- 2 tbsp melted butter
- 1 tbsp lemon juice

Instructions:

1. Whisk flour, sugar, baking powder, baking soda, and salt.
2. In another bowl, combine ricotta, buttermilk, eggs, lemon zest, lemon juice, and melted butter.
3. Fold wet into dry until just combined.
4. Cook pancakes on medium griddle until golden.

Pumpkin Spice Pancakes

Ingredients:

- Use Classic Buttermilk Pancake batter
- ½ cup canned pumpkin puree
- 1 tsp pumpkin pie spice
- ½ tsp cinnamon

Instructions:

1. Stir pumpkin puree and spices into batter.
2. Cook pancakes as usual.

Apple Cinnamon Pancakes

Ingredients:

- Use Classic Buttermilk Pancake batter
- 1 apple, peeled and finely diced
- 1 tsp cinnamon

Instructions:

1. Fold diced apple and cinnamon into batter.
2. Cook pancakes on griddle until golden.

Oatmeal Pancakes

Ingredients:

- 1 cup rolled oats
- 1 cup all-purpose flour
- 2 tbsp sugar
- 1 tsp baking powder
- 1 tsp baking soda
- ½ tsp salt
- 1 ½ cups buttermilk
- 1 large egg
- 3 tbsp melted butter

Instructions:

1. In a bowl, mix oats, flour, sugar, baking powder, baking soda, and salt.
2. Whisk buttermilk, egg, and melted butter in another bowl.
3. Combine wet and dry ingredients. Let batter sit 5-10 mins to soften oats.
4. Cook pancakes as usual.

Whole Wheat Pancakes

Ingredients:

- 1 cup whole wheat flour
- 1 tbsp sugar
- 1 tsp baking powder
- ½ tsp baking soda
- ¼ tsp salt
- 1 cup buttermilk (or milk)
- 1 large egg
- 2 tbsp melted butter or oil

Instructions:

1. Whisk flour, sugar, baking powder, baking soda, and salt.
2. In another bowl, mix buttermilk, egg, and melted butter.
3. Combine wet and dry ingredients, stir until just combined.
4. Cook on a greased griddle over medium heat until bubbles form, then flip.

Strawberry Pancakes

Ingredients:

- Use your favorite pancake batter (classic or whole wheat)
- 1 cup fresh sliced strawberries

Instructions:

1. Gently fold strawberries into batter just before cooking.
2. Cook pancakes as usual.

Sweet Potato Pancakes

Ingredients:

- 1 cup mashed cooked sweet potato
- 1 cup flour
- 1 tbsp sugar
- 1 tsp baking powder
- ½ tsp baking soda
- ¼ tsp salt
- 1 cup milk or buttermilk
- 1 large egg
- 2 tbsp melted butter

Instructions:

1. Mix flour, sugar, baking powder, soda, and salt.
2. Whisk mashed sweet potato, milk, egg, and butter.
3. Combine wet and dry ingredients until just mixed.
4. Cook pancakes on griddle until golden.

Gluten-Free Pancakes

Ingredients:

- 1 cup gluten-free flour blend
- 1 tbsp sugar
- 1 tsp baking powder
- ½ tsp baking soda
- ¼ tsp salt
- 1 cup milk or dairy-free milk
- 1 large egg
- 2 tbsp melted butter or oil

Instructions:

1. Mix dry ingredients in a bowl.
2. Whisk wet ingredients separately.
3. Combine and stir until just combined.
4. Cook on medium heat until bubbles appear, then flip.

Vegan Pancakes

Ingredients:

- 1 cup all-purpose or whole wheat flour
- 1 tbsp sugar
- 1 tbsp baking powder
- ¼ tsp salt
- 1 cup plant-based milk (almond, soy, oat)
- 2 tbsp vegetable oil
- 1 tsp vanilla extract

Instructions:

1. Mix flour, sugar, baking powder, and salt.
2. Whisk plant milk, oil, and vanilla.
3. Combine wet and dry ingredients gently.
4. Cook on lightly greased griddle until bubbles form, flip carefully.

Crepes with Nutella

Ingredients:

- 1 cup all-purpose flour
- 2 large eggs
- 1 ½ cups milk
- 2 tbsp melted butter
- 1 tbsp sugar
- Pinch of salt
- Nutella for filling

Instructions:

1. Whisk flour, eggs, milk, melted butter, sugar, and salt until smooth.
2. Let batter rest 20 minutes in fridge.
3. Heat non-stick pan over medium heat, lightly grease.
4. Pour about ¼ cup batter, swirl to thinly coat pan.
5. Cook ~1-2 minutes, flip, cook 30 seconds more.
6. Spread Nutella inside crepe, fold or roll, and serve.

Buckwheat Pancakes

Ingredients:

- 1 cup buckwheat flour
- 1 cup all-purpose flour
- 2 tbsp sugar
- 1 tsp baking powder
- ½ tsp baking soda
- ¼ tsp salt
- 1 ¼ cups buttermilk
- 2 large eggs
- 3 tbsp melted butter

Instructions:

1. Mix dry ingredients in a bowl.
2. Whisk buttermilk, eggs, and butter separately.
3. Combine wet and dry until just mixed.
4. Cook on griddle until bubbly and golden.

Cornmeal Pancakes

Ingredients:

- ¾ cup cornmeal
- ¾ cup all-purpose flour
- 1 tbsp sugar
- 1 tsp baking powder
- ½ tsp baking soda
- ¼ tsp salt
- 1 ¼ cups buttermilk or milk
- 1 large egg
- 2 tbsp melted butter

Instructions:

1. Mix cornmeal, flour, sugar, baking powder, baking soda, and salt.
2. Whisk buttermilk, egg, and butter separately.
3. Combine until just mixed.
4. Cook on greased skillet over medium heat until golden.

Ricotta and Honey Pancakes

Ingredients:

- 1 cup all-purpose flour
- 1 tbsp sugar
- 1 tsp baking powder
- ¼ tsp salt
- 1 cup milk
- 1 large egg
- ½ cup ricotta cheese
- 2 tbsp honey, plus extra for drizzling
- 2 tbsp melted butter

Instructions:

1. In a bowl, whisk flour, sugar, baking powder, and salt.
2. In another bowl, mix milk, egg, ricotta, honey, and melted butter.
3. Combine wet and dry ingredients gently.
4. Cook pancakes on a greased griddle until bubbles form, then flip and cook until golden.
5. Serve drizzled with extra honey.

Peanut Butter Pancakes

Ingredients:

- 1 cup all-purpose flour
- 1 tbsp sugar
- 1 tsp baking powder
- ¼ tsp salt
- 1 cup milk
- 1 large egg
- ¼ cup creamy peanut butter
- 2 tbsp melted butter

Instructions:

1. Mix flour, sugar, baking powder, and salt.
2. In a separate bowl, whisk milk, egg, peanut butter, and melted butter until smooth.
3. Combine wet and dry ingredients until just mixed.
4. Cook on medium heat until bubbles appear, flip and cook through.

Cinnamon Roll Pancakes

Ingredients:

- 1 cup all-purpose flour
- 1 tbsp sugar
- 1 tsp baking powder
- ½ tsp ground cinnamon
- ¼ tsp salt
- 1 cup milk
- 1 large egg
- 2 tbsp melted butter

Cinnamon Swirl:

- 3 tbsp melted butter
- 2 tbsp brown sugar
- 1 tsp cinnamon

Instructions:

1. Mix flour, sugar, baking powder, cinnamon, and salt.
2. Whisk milk, egg, and melted butter separately.
3. Combine wet and dry ingredients.

4. For each pancake, pour batter on griddle, then drizzle a mixture of melted butter, brown sugar, and cinnamon in a swirl pattern.

5. Cook until bubbles form, flip carefully, and cook until golden.

Sourdough Pancakes

Ingredients:

- 1 cup sourdough starter (unfed or discard)
- 1 cup all-purpose flour
- 1 cup milk
- 1 large egg
- 2 tbsp sugar
- 2 tbsp melted butter
- 1 tsp baking soda
- ¼ tsp salt

Instructions:

1. Mix sourdough starter, flour, milk, egg, sugar, and melted butter.
2. Let sit 10 minutes.
3. Just before cooking, stir in baking soda and salt.
4. Cook pancakes on a greased griddle over medium heat until bubbly, then flip and cook until golden.

Carrot Cake Pancakes

Ingredients:

- 1 cup all-purpose flour
- 1 tbsp sugar
- 1 tsp baking powder
- ½ tsp cinnamon
- ¼ tsp nutmeg
- ¼ tsp salt
- 1 cup grated carrot
- 1 cup milk
- 1 large egg
- 2 tbsp melted butter
- ½ cup chopped walnuts or pecans (optional)

Instructions:

1. Mix flour, sugar, baking powder, cinnamon, nutmeg, and salt.
2. In another bowl, whisk milk, egg, and melted butter.
3. Combine wet and dry ingredients, fold in grated carrot and nuts.
4. Cook pancakes until bubbles form, flip, and cook until golden.

Lemon Poppy Seed Pancakes

Ingredients:

- 1 cup all-purpose flour
- 2 tbsp sugar
- 1 tsp baking powder
- ¼ tsp salt
- 1 tbsp poppy seeds
- Zest of 1 lemon
- 1 cup milk
- 1 large egg
- 2 tbsp melted butter
- 1 tbsp lemon juice

Instructions:

1. Whisk flour, sugar, baking powder, salt, poppy seeds, and lemon zest.
2. In another bowl, combine milk, egg, melted butter, and lemon juice.
3. Mix wet and dry ingredients gently.
4. Cook on medium heat until bubbles appear, flip and cook through.

Bacon Pancakes

Ingredients:

- 1 cup all-purpose flour
- 1 tbsp sugar
- 1 tsp baking powder
- ¼ tsp salt
- 1 cup milk
- 1 large egg
- 2 tbsp melted butter
- 6 strips cooked bacon, chopped

Instructions:

1. Mix flour, sugar, baking powder, and salt.
2. Whisk milk, egg, and melted butter.
3. Combine wet and dry ingredients. Fold in bacon pieces.
4. Cook pancakes until golden and cooked through.

Savory Herb Pancakes

Ingredients:

- 1 cup all-purpose flour
- 1 tsp baking powder
- ½ tsp salt
- 2 tbsp chopped fresh herbs (chives, parsley, thyme)
- 1 cup milk
- 1 large egg
- 2 tbsp melted butter
- Optional: ¼ cup grated Parmesan cheese

Instructions:

1. Combine flour, baking powder, salt, herbs, and cheese if using.
2. Whisk milk, egg, and butter.
3. Mix wet and dry ingredients gently.
4. Cook on medium heat until edges set and bubbles appear, flip and cook until done.

Chive and Cheese Pancakes

Ingredients:

- 1 cup all-purpose flour
- 1 tsp baking powder
- ½ tsp salt
- 2 tbsp chopped fresh chives
- ½ cup shredded cheddar or your favorite cheese
- 1 cup milk
- 1 large egg
- 2 tbsp melted butter

Instructions:

1. In a bowl, mix flour, baking powder, salt, chives, and cheese.
2. In another bowl, whisk milk, egg, and melted butter.
3. Combine wet and dry ingredients gently.
4. Cook pancakes on a hot greased griddle until bubbles form, then flip and cook until golden and cooked through.

Maple Syrup Glazed Bacon

Ingredients:

- 12 slices thick-cut bacon
- ½ cup pure maple syrup

Instructions:

1. Preheat oven to 400°F (200°C).
2. Lay bacon strips on a foil-lined baking sheet.
3. Brush maple syrup generously over bacon slices.
4. Bake for 15–20 minutes or until crispy and caramelized, brushing more syrup halfway through.
5. Let cool slightly before serving.

Honey Butter Syrup

Ingredients:

- ¼ cup unsalted butter
- ¼ cup honey
- 2 tbsp maple syrup (optional)

Instructions:

1. In a small saucepan, melt butter over low heat.
2. Stir in honey and maple syrup until well combined and warm.
3. Serve warm drizzled over pancakes.

Blueberry Maple Syrup

Ingredients:

- 1 cup fresh or frozen blueberries
- ½ cup pure maple syrup
- 1 tbsp lemon juice

Instructions:

1. In a small saucepan, combine blueberries, maple syrup, and lemon juice.
2. Simmer over medium heat for 5–7 minutes, mashing some berries as it cooks.
3. Remove from heat and let cool slightly.
4. Serve warm over pancakes.

Cinnamon Maple Syrup

Ingredients:

- 1 cup pure maple syrup
- 1 tsp ground cinnamon
- ½ tsp vanilla extract (optional)

Instructions:

1. Warm maple syrup in a saucepan over low heat.
2. Whisk in cinnamon and vanilla extract until fully combined.
3. Serve warm over pancakes.

Bourbon Maple Syrup

Ingredients:

- 1 cup pure maple syrup
- 2 tbsp bourbon
- 1 tsp vanilla extract

Instructions:

1. Warm maple syrup in a saucepan over low heat.
2. Stir in bourbon and vanilla extract until combined.
3. Serve warm for an adult twist on pancakes.

Pumpkin Spice Syrup

Ingredients:

- 1 cup pure maple syrup
- 1 tsp pumpkin pie spice
- ½ tsp vanilla extract

Instructions:

1. Heat maple syrup in a saucepan on low heat.
2. Whisk in pumpkin pie spice and vanilla extract.
3. Simmer for 2-3 minutes, then serve warm.

Strawberry Compote

Ingredients:

- 2 cups fresh strawberries, hulled and halved
- ¼ cup sugar
- 1 tbsp lemon juice
- 1 tsp vanilla extract

Instructions:

1. Combine strawberries, sugar, and lemon juice in a saucepan over medium heat.
2. Cook, stirring occasionally, until strawberries release juices and soften (about 10 minutes).
3. Stir in vanilla extract and remove from heat.
4. Serve warm or room temperature over pancakes.

Mixed Berry Syrup

Ingredients:

- 1 cup mixed berries (fresh or frozen)
- ½ cup sugar
- ½ cup water
- 1 tsp lemon juice

Instructions:

1. Combine berries, sugar, and water in a saucepan over medium heat.
2. Bring to a simmer and cook for 10–15 minutes until berries break down and syrup thickens slightly.
3. Stir in lemon juice.
4. Strain if desired for a smooth syrup or leave chunky. Serve warm or cold.

Apple Cider Syrup

Ingredients:

- 1 cup apple cider
- ½ cup brown sugar
- 1 tsp cinnamon

Instructions:

1. Combine apple cider, brown sugar, and cinnamon in a saucepan.
2. Simmer over medium heat until syrup reduces by half and thickens (about 15–20 minutes).
3. Cool slightly before serving.

Ginger Syrup

Ingredients:

- 1 cup water
- 1 cup sugar
- 2-inch piece fresh ginger, peeled and sliced

Instructions:

1. Combine water, sugar, and ginger in a saucepan.
2. Bring to a boil, then reduce heat and simmer for 15 minutes.
3. Remove from heat and let steep for another 10 minutes.
4. Strain out ginger slices. Serve warm or chilled.

Vanilla Bean Syrup

Ingredients:

- 1 cup water
- 1 cup sugar
- 1 vanilla bean, split lengthwise

Instructions:

1. Combine water, sugar, and vanilla bean (including seeds) in a saucepan.
2. Bring to a boil, then reduce heat and simmer for 5 minutes.
3. Remove from heat, cool, and remove vanilla bean.
4. Store in a bottle and use as desired.

Pecan Maple Syrup

Ingredients:

- 1 cup pure maple syrup
- ½ cup chopped pecans
- 1 tbsp butter

Instructions:

1. In a small saucepan, gently warm maple syrup and butter.
2. Stir in chopped pecans and simmer for 5 minutes to infuse flavor.
3. Serve warm over pancakes.

Orange Blossom Syrup

Ingredients:

- 1 cup water
- 1 cup sugar
- 2 tbsp orange blossom water
- Zest of 1 orange

Instructions:

1. Combine water, sugar, and orange zest in a saucepan.
2. Bring to a boil, then simmer until syrup thickens slightly (about 10 minutes).
3. Remove from heat, stir in orange blossom water.
4. Cool and strain before serving.

Blackberry Syrup

Ingredients:

- 1 cup blackberries
- ½ cup sugar
- ½ cup water
- 1 tsp lemon juice

Instructions:

1. Combine blackberries, sugar, and water in a saucepan.
2. Simmer for 10–15 minutes, mashing berries to release juice.
3. Stir in lemon juice.
4. Strain if desired. Serve warm or chilled.

Lemon Syrup

Ingredients:

- 1 cup water
- 1 cup sugar
- ½ cup fresh lemon juice
- Zest of 1 lemon

Instructions:

1. Combine water, sugar, and lemon zest in a saucepan.
2. Bring to a boil, then simmer until sugar dissolves and syrup thickens slightly (5–7 minutes).
3. Remove from heat, stir in lemon juice.
4. Cool and strain before serving.

Chocolate Syrup

Ingredients:

- 1 cup cocoa powder
- 1 cup sugar
- 1 cup water
- 1 tsp vanilla extract
- Pinch of salt

Instructions:

1. In a saucepan, whisk together cocoa powder and sugar.
2. Add water slowly, stirring to combine.
3. Bring mixture to a boil over medium heat, then reduce to a simmer.
4. Stir constantly for 3–5 minutes until thickened.
5. Remove from heat, stir in vanilla and salt. Cool before serving.

Caramel Syrup

Ingredients:

- 1 cup sugar
- 6 tbsp butter (unsalted)
- ½ cup heavy cream
- Pinch of salt

Instructions:

1. Heat sugar in a saucepan over medium heat, stirring constantly until it melts and turns a deep amber color.
2. Remove from heat and quickly add butter, stirring until melted.
3. Slowly add heavy cream while stirring (mixture will bubble).
4. Stir in salt. Let cool slightly before serving.

Bacon and Maple Syrup Pancakes

Ingredients:

- Your favorite pancake batter
- Cooked crispy bacon strips
- Maple syrup

Instructions:

1. Cook pancakes as usual.
2. Layer crispy bacon strips on top of pancakes or fold into batter before cooking.
3. Drizzle with warm maple syrup. Serve immediately.

Pancakes with Whipped Cream and Berries

Ingredients:

- Pancakes
- Whipped cream (homemade or store-bought)
- Fresh mixed berries (strawberries, blueberries, raspberries)

Instructions:

1. Stack pancakes on a plate.
2. Top with generous dollops of whipped cream.
3. Scatter fresh berries over the top. Serve immediately.

Pancake Stack with Nut Butter

Ingredients:

- Pancakes
- Your favorite nut butter (peanut, almond, cashew)
- Honey or maple syrup (optional)

Instructions:

1. Spread a layer of nut butter between each pancake in the stack.
2. Drizzle honey or maple syrup on top if desired.
3. Serve warm.

Sweet Potato Hash

Ingredients:

- 2 large sweet potatoes, peeled and diced
- 1 small onion, diced
- 1 bell pepper, diced
- 2 cloves garlic, minced
- 2 tbsp olive oil
- Salt and pepper to taste
- Optional: chopped fresh parsley or cilantro

Instructions:

1. Heat olive oil in a large skillet over medium heat.
2. Add sweet potatoes and cook for 8–10 minutes, stirring occasionally until they begin to soften.
3. Add onion, bell pepper, and garlic; cook another 5–7 minutes until vegetables are tender and slightly caramelized.
4. Season with salt and pepper. Garnish with fresh herbs if desired. Serve warm alongside pancakes.

Breakfast Burrito with Pancakes

Ingredients:

- Pancakes (medium size)
- 2 eggs, scrambled or fried
- 2 sausage links or patties, cooked and sliced
- ¼ cup shredded cheese (cheddar or your choice)
- Salsa or hot sauce (optional)
- Fresh cilantro (optional)

Instructions:

1. Cook pancakes as usual, keep warm.
2. Cook eggs to your liking (scrambled or fried).
3. Warm sausages and slice.
4. On each pancake, layer eggs, sausage, and cheese.
5. Add salsa or hot sauce if desired.
6. Roll the pancake up like a burrito, folding in the sides to hold filling.
7. Garnish with cilantro and serve immediately.

Pancakes with Fried Eggs and Sausage

Ingredients:

- Pancakes
- 2 eggs, fried sunny side up or over easy
- 2 breakfast sausage links or patties, cooked

Instructions:

1. Prepare pancakes and keep warm.
2. Fry eggs as desired.
3. Cook sausage until browned and cooked through.
4. Serve pancakes topped or alongside with fried eggs and sausage.

Pancakes with Greek Yogurt and Honey

Ingredients:

- Pancakes
- ½ cup Greek yogurt
- 2 tbsp honey
- Optional: fresh berries or nuts for topping

Instructions:

1. Make pancakes and keep warm.
2. Spoon Greek yogurt over pancakes.
3. Drizzle honey generously on top.
4. Add fresh berries or nuts if desired. Serve immediately.

Pancakes with Fresh Fruit Salad

Ingredients:

- Pancakes
- Mixed fresh fruit salad (e.g., diced strawberries, blueberries, kiwi, banana, mango)
- Optional: a sprinkle of powdered sugar or a drizzle of maple syrup

Instructions:

1. Prepare pancakes and keep warm.
2. Toss fresh fruits in a bowl.
3. Serve pancakes topped with a generous portion of fresh fruit salad.
4. Add powdered sugar or maple syrup on top if desired.

www.ingramcontent.com/pod-product-compliance
Lightning Source LLC
LaVergne TN
LVHW081327060526
838201LV00055B/2495